COACHING 6, 7 AND 8 YEAR OLDS

By

Tony Waiters

With

Bobby Howe

World of Soccer Ltd.
Vancouver

First published 1988 by WORLD OF SOCCER

Phone: (604) 921-8963 Fax: (604) 921-8964
Information Service: 1-800-762-2378

CREDITS
Editor: Bob Dunn
Illustrator: Martin Nichols
Copy Processing: Barbara Schiffner
Layout and Design: Dunn Communications Ltd.

Manufactured by Hemlock Printers Ltd.

Canadian Cataloguing in Publication Data
Waiters, Tony
    Coaching 6, 7 and 8 year olds : micro soccer
ISBN 1-896466-01-X
1. Soccer for children – Coaching.
I. Howe, Bobby II. Nichols, Martin III. Title.
IV. Title: Coaching six, seven and eight year olds.
V. Title: Micro soccer.
GV943.8.WS4 1995 796.334'07'7 C95-900464-5

First printing June, 1988
Second printing April, 1989
Third printing January, 1991
Fourth printing May, 1992
Fifth printing April, 1993
Sixth printing September, 1993
Seventh printing May, 1995
Eighth printing April, 1996
Ninth printing July, 1997
Tenth printing May, 1998
Eleventh printing Sept, 1998

Twelfth printing July, 1999
Thirteenth printing August, 2000

THE COACHING SERIES:

Coaching 6, 7 and 8 year olds

Coaching 9, 10 and 11 year olds

Coaching the Team

Coaching the Goalkeeper

Coaching the Player

OTHER WORLD OF SOCCER PUBLICATIONS:

Teaching Offside

Soccer is Fun – 1!, 2! & 3! – A Workbook for 6, 7 and 8 Year Olds

Hotshots! – 1, 2 & 3 – A Workbook for 9, 10 and 11 Year Olds

Micro Soccer – Rules & Regulations

Coaching to Win

Total Player Development™

Ace Coaching Cards

Zonal Defending

ACKNOWLEDGEMENTS

Sheila Adams
Jack Gill
Gerry Harrington
Dick Howard
Earl LaBounty
Jim Le Nobel
John McKenzie
Ken Morton
Blair Murdoch
Stu Watson

DEDICATION

This book is dedicated to a very special group of people — the most important and influential people in soccer. It is for the countless Moms and Dads who take upon themselves the responsibility of coaching the youngest soccer players.

TABLE OF CONTENTS

INTRODUCTION

This manual is not about professional soccer. It is for the coaches of 6, 7 and 8-year-olds — and the authors can speak with authority, from experience. The records of both Tony Waiters and Bobby Howe at the professional level are impressive. But it is also in the less visible areas of the game that Waiters and Howe have considerable experience.

Waiters is one of an elite group of International Coaches conducting the FIFA WORLD YOUTH FOOTBALL ACADEMY around the globe. The Academy looks at the different considerations for youth coaches at age levels from Under-6 through to Under-18.

While employed by the English Football Association, much of Waiters work was with youth coaches and teachers, during which time he coached a pilot group of 8-year-olds for a full year. Since his involvement in the 1986 World Cup in Mexico, Waiters has spent much of his coaching time with 6-year-olds and their coaches. His work in *Micro Soccer* has led to clinics for coaches and their young players on four continents.

Howe's position as State Youth Coach for Washington means he's in daily contact with coaches of young soccer players in the Pacific Northwest. He has dedicated a significant portion of his efforts to the development of modified, or *Mod-Soccer*, in the United States. His responsibilities as a United States Soccer Federation Instructor include making recommendations for the content of the Federation's D, E and F licenses — with an emphasis on youth soccer.

Waiters describes Howe as "the best coach of young players I have ever seen."

Special Considerations

For 6, 7 and 8-year-olds

- The boys and girls must be regarded as young children — not mini-adults.

- Because they are still so young and essentially self-orientated, they relate naturally to a friend or two and not to large groups of six or more.

- They cannot sustain prolonged activity and function best in fits and starts.

- Their concentration span is limited, so frequent changes of pace and activity are necessary.

- The fun and activity factors must always be kept in mind. *Remember*: children love to learn, so skills development, team play and co-operation are important. They form the *core* of every practice.

The difference between 6, 7 and 8-year-olds

The reason why this manual is called "Coaching 6, 7 and 8-year-olds" and not "Coaching 6 to 8-year-olds" is to stress the different stages in growth, development and skills learning that take place over three years. From 6 to 7 to 8 is almost a lifetime for kids! All children are individuals and develop in different ways, and at different stages, so coaches are still compelled to talk in general terms. For simplicity, consider the 6-year-olds as first-year players, and 7 and 8-year-olds as the second and third-year players, respectively.

Year One (6-year-olds)

The emphasis is on *playing*. Formal skills learning has little relevance to these young soccer minds. Game activities such as 3-a-side play or other fun situations where each player has a ball are strongly recommended. Only introduce more technique-oriented practices when it is apparent they have developed the desire — through play — to improve their skills.

Year Two (7-year-olds)

By now, young players have become familiar with soccer and "handling" the ball — both with feet and hands. More formal skills learning can now take place. Remain cautious about using drills that have players waiting in line. While more structured exercises are good for developing the essential skills, be aware the concentration level of these players is low. If possible, split the group into two (it would be helpful to have an assistant) and work two groups at once; or one group on skills practice while the other plays a game. Then rotate the groups. Periodically introduce larger numbers into the end-of-session scrimmage . . . e.g., 4 and 5-a-side, but use 3-a-side as the basic format.

Year Three (8-year-olds)

Although the requirements don't change much — kids still want to play and kick a soccer ball — the third season should see them eager to develop their skills. The whole range of the *Micro Soccer* system and the Bobby Howe practices outlined in this manual should be used to help satisfy that desire. Remember that at least half — ideally more — of each session should be in a game form: 3-a-side or 4-a-side. Be aware of the programs they will be graduating to . . . i.e., 7-a-side, 8-a-side and, eventually, 11-a-side and prepare them for it (throw-ins, penalties, free kicks, offside). But don't become too concerned about moving them up into the 'larger' games too fast — for all the reasons stated in this manual.

Why a book for coaching 6, 7 and 8-year-olds?

- Little research and attention has been applied to this critical growth period in soccer.
- Limited relevant information is presently available.
- All educators agree — the early learning experiences are the most important and produce the most retention.
- Most coaches are parents who volunteer their services, often at the last minute, and few possess previous coaching or soccer experience, or the time to attend Certification Courses.
- Traditionally, soccer programs for the beginning player have been viewed from an adult perspective with the 11-a-side game as the reference point.

This manual starts with the novice player and progresses from there, at the child's pace and for the benefit of the child. However, it does consider those special people — the Moms and Dads — who coach the "team". They deserve a manual which will guarantee success, achieved through the enjoyment of their children and the kids' visible improvement in soccer skills.

This manual will help to achieve that objective.

Why a new way of coaching 6, 7 and 8-year-olds?

- For too long, the children's game of soccer has been a diluted version of the adult game. Novice players have been regarded as small adults — not young children.
- Almost half of the youngsters currently playing soccer in North America are in this age group.
- Until recently, young players in North America and Europe began playing organized soccer in the 11-a-side game. The only concessions were in the scaling down of the field dimensions and, sometimes, the size of the goals.
- Kids want to kick the ball. In 11 vs 11, there is ONE ball among 22 players.
- During the last decade, in both the United States and Canada, smaller numbers in team play have been implemented. Most 6-year-olds are now playing 7 or 8-a-side soccer — called *Mod-Soccer* in U.S.A. and *Mini-Soccer* in Canada. One ball among 14 players on scaled-down fields represents *real* progress.
- Even in 7-a-side soccer, the "swarm" effect continues. All youngsters try to kick the ball — and why shouldn't they?

Mini and *Mod-Soccer* have produced an important breakthrough in introducing the game to novice players.

But. . . THERE IS A COMPELLING NEED TO REDUCE NUMBERS EVEN FURTHER, ESPECIALLY IN PRACTICE.

HOW TO USE

You are a *Coach*. The kids need you and are looking for activity and fun. You must meet their expectations and those of their parents, too.

People, and clubs, will acquire this book to help the coaches of our young players to do just that — to coach.

That is how the book *should* be used.

All the information required to guarantee a successful, enjoyable soccer practice is contained on pages 10 to 29.

Coaches should study those pages first. By the time you have finished page 29, you will be equipped to run a successful practice.

The Bobby Howe segment — starting on page 39 — shows another 10 excellent practices for 6, 7 and 8-year-olds. They should be introduced when players have become familiar with *Micro Soccer* and its accompanying practices. Coaches who are into their second or third season of coaching the same group of players in this age range will find Bobby's practices invaluable. They will produce a great deal of fun and improvement in skills.

The Appendix – pages 51 to 64 – contains relevant information in the coaching of 6, 7 and 8-year-olds; also the rationale behind the Waitersway Coaching Methods; and how *Micro Soccer* is much more than a system just for 6, 7 and 8-year-olds. This part of the manual should be read at your leisure.

This book should help *every* coach of beginner players. Use it for your benefit, and therefore for the benefit of your young players.

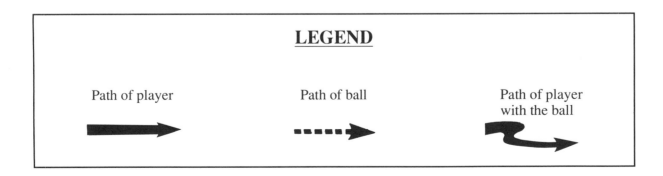

LEGEND

Path of player	Path of ball	Path of player with the ball

MICRO SOCCER

What is *Micro Soccer*?

Micro Soccer is 3-a-side soccer, the Waitersway. It uses simple game rules that will be explained on the pages that follow. Of the three players on each team one is a goalkeeper, although the player in goal is changed frequently — on a rotating basis.

The practices of *Micro Soccer* use the *Micro Soccer* field to assist in the organization of the practices. The 10 *Micro Soccer* practices are fun games, and fun drills that specifically develop the essential basic skills of soccer.

Micro Soccer and its practices have been developed to give the coach of the novice player a simple formula that guarantees fun, skills development and a fundamental knowledge of soccer in such a way that a child of 6, 7 or 8 years of age can understand.

The base is 3-a-side

- A 6-year-old relates to and co-operates with one or two friends (accepted educational psychology).

- One ball among 6 guarantees the opportunity for all players to kick, dribble — and score!

- Three makes the triangle — the basic team unit of soccer.

- The 3-a-side game has always been played *naturally* by youngsters around the world. The great players have developed from this type of environment.

- Children do not play *naturally* in Canada and the United States. *Street soccer* is not a part of the North American society's sports mosaic.

- The *Waitersway* of coaching for 6, 7 and 8-year-olds uses Tony Waiters' own 3-a-side game with 10 other standard fun practices based on the 3-a-side game. The practices produce skills development *just by playing*. To quote Bobby Howe: "The game is the great teacher".

Introducing *Micro Soccer*

When players are being introduced to *Micro Soccer* for the first time, you cannot expect everything to go perfectly.

The teaching of the game and the organization of the practices will require time for everyone to familiarize themselves with the requirements. After a few weeks, however, there should be no difficulties.

Do not be deterred. The principles are right. The game is right. Persist. The rewards will be there for all, and particularly for the players, after a short period of time.

Why 3-a-side?

Why not 1 vs 1, or 2 vs 2?

The basic team unit of soccer is three. The triangle forms the basic tactical configuration. An attacker with the ball should have at least TWO passing options.

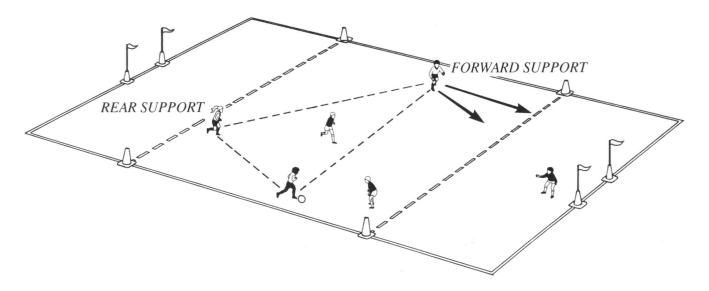

Forward support gives the player a creative, positive passing option. Rear support gives the player insurance, in case a mistake is made or the player with the ball cannot use the front supporting player but wishes to pass.

Why not 4-a-side?

The 4-a-side game is good but . . .

Watch 6-year-olds playing 7-a-side soccer. When they swarm for the ball, there are still "passengers" on the field. "Playing positions" is for the birds — or the adults. Why "play position" to get an occasional kick at the ball?

Some players are non-assertive, others non-physical, still others limited in skill. While 7-a-side will definitely leave them on the outside looking in, 4-a-side is only an improvement. One player will often be excluded, either by choice or uncertainty. But 3-a-side soccer eliminates this. Every player has an easily understood role which *guarantees* involvement.

There is nothing revolutionary about the *Micro Soccer* game or its practices. It might be regarded as the BGO — Blinding Glimpse of the Obvious! It only needs a formalizing of the 'natural' game and its practices.

For the first time, a method of introducing soccer has been devised which looks specifically at the needs of the beginning player. It *starts there* — and progresses from that base, growing and developing as the player does, into the adult game.

Until now, the reverse has been true. The game has been presented as a watered-down version of the adult game. The reduction in scale has been the only concession to the small, *6-year-old adult.*

Micro Soccer, 3-a-side. Welcome to the game of the kids. They're bound to enjoy it. And they're *certain* to be involved.

Micro Soccer and its organization

Micro Soccer is used to distinguish the game beyond that of small-sided games, mini-soccer and mod-soccer. *Micro Soccer* uses the fundamental team unit — three — as the basis for learning and for having fun.

There are variations in the way 3-a-side soccer can be played. Some are presented in this manual. The rules of *Micro Soccer* and its organization are covered on the next two pages.

The rules of *Micro Soccer*

1. The field is approximately 30 yards x 20 yards although the size can be adjusted over a period of time by trial and error. The dimensions should vary according to the age and abilities of the players. If it is not possible to line the fields, use existing field markings, cones and/or frisbees.

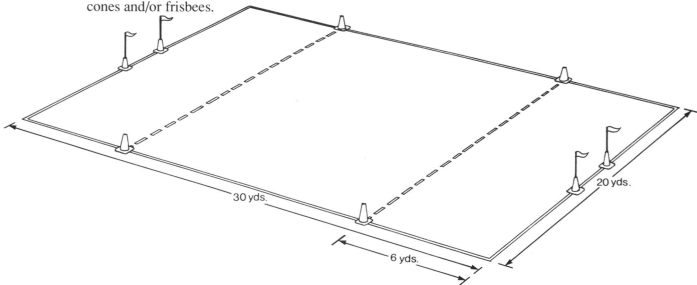

2. If the field is not lined, marker cones are placed on the sidelines, six yards out from goal lines. These mark an imaginary line forming the goalkeeping zone. The goalkeeper can handle the ball inside this zone, but may play (and should be encouraged to do so) beyond the line in a conventional manner, using feet and body but not the hands.

3. Goals are set up using corner flags (preferably free-standing ones), nine feet apart. An ideal method is to use poles or corner flags inserted in large cones.

4. Goals can be scored from anywhere but the ball must pass below the imaginary line across the top of goals.

5. The coach referees, or appoints his assistant or a parent.

6. Time-outs are called every two or three minutes, when substitutions are made.

7. Each team has a goalkeeper, but the goalkeepers are changed at each time-out on a rotating basis so that "equal time" is established for the goalkeeping function.

8. If there are six players on a team (three on, three off), line changes can be made periodically so the same three players do not always play together.

9. When the ball goes out of play, the game is re-started by one of the following ways:

   a) Over the sidelines, with a throw-in (or kick-in, if the coach so desires).

   b) Over the goal line, with a goal kick if attacking team last touched the ball; or corner kick if defending team last played ball (goal kick is taken from anywhere in the goalkeeper handing zone; corner from where goal line and sideline meet).

   c) After a goal is scored, re-start the game with a goal kick. Alternatively, with the youngest players, mark a center spot, and re-start with a kick-off from the center.

   Note: Goals cannot be scored directly from a goal kick, a throw-in, a kick off or a free kick. There are no penalty kicks in *Micro Soccer*.

10. If a foul throw is committed, the coach explains the correct method and lets the offender re-take the throw. Discretionary power is then given to the referee if another foul throw is committed but, most times, it won't be called.

11. Because of the small field size and the end-to-end nature of the game, the ball may go out of play frequently. Coaches should encourage parents to participate as *ball parents* to help the flow and the enjoyment of the game. Any players on the sidelines should be encouraged to help get the ball back in play quickly. On gymnasia, artificial turf, all-weather and other hard surfaces the ball will run more quickly. If possible, compensate by widening the playing area or by reducing the air pressure of the ball.

12. Practice sessions (and games) are *no longer* than 35 to 40 minutes. Because of this, parents are encouraged to stay for both practices and games and to participate in practice sessions.

13. All infringements — tripping handling, etc. — are punished by an indirect free kick, i.e. ball must be passed first before a shot can be taken. There are no penalties (players of this age are completely honest and do not commit deliberate fouls; and the 'indirect' free kick encourages passing and co-operation).

14. All opposing players must be at least five yards from the ball on free kicks, corner kicks and goal kicks.

Please Note: A more comprehensive and formalized Micro Soccer Rule Book for Tournament and Match Play is available from the publishers.

System for substitutions and rotation

A substitution or rotation system will depend on the number of players available:

With 3 players — There are no substitutes. Increase the number of time-outs and reduce playing time of game. Remember about "equal time" for goalkeepers. Because the game's intensity is, for young players, impossible to sustain for a long period, a two-minute system is most effective. The ideal "practice" number.

With 4 players — One substitute. The sequence is the goalkeeper becomes the substitute, substitute becomes the outfield player and one outfield player becomes the goalkeeper.

With 5 players — An awkward number. The two substitutes always come back on the field as the two outfield players; one of the previous outfield players becomes a substitute — the other the goalkeeper; the replaced goalkeeper becomes the other substitute. Each rotation must have equal time and equal goalkeeping time must be maintained.

With 6 players — The perfect substitute system. With three on three off, there is a different goalkeeper each time and when all six have played goal, repeat the procedure. Make line changes periodically. A 6-player system is good for games and tournaments, but is not enough acitivty for practice situations.

EQUIPMENT

Posts 4'6"to 5'
— corner flags
or plastic pipes

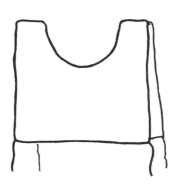

Bibs, or sashes
for goalkeeper
identification

Markers for
improvising field

Supporting cones
for posts

Triangular cones

Wosmarkers

One ball per player

Marker cones
for goal areas

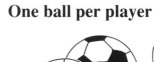

A FEAST

The coach's objectives for 6, 7 and 8-year-olds

The aim in every practice is to give the boys and girls plenty of action . . .

Fun — has to be an essential requirement of every exercise, at every practice.

Everyone — must receive an equal opportunity of involvement — in other words, equal time.

Activity — must be at the core of the soccer sessions, because it affects every other part of the FEAST.

Skills — must be developed for greater enjoyment of soccer, through greater accomplishment.

Team play — must be included in every activity, because soccer is a 'team' game.

So you give the players a *FEAST*. And whether the main course is the tastiest pizza or the sweetest of sports, you have to avoid giving them too much to digest.

MICRO SOCCER PRACTICES

Square Dance

Objective

To start practice in a lively way with a fun warm-up that introduces and develops the fundamentals of dribbling.

Organization

- Mark a square approximately 15 yards by 15 yards, depending on numbers.

- Each player should have a ball.

- If not, use the "Change Soccer" principle: half the players inside the square each with a ball, half outside without a ball. Trade places on shout "Change!"

- Three instructions are given to the players inside the square:

  "STOP" Put foot on top of ball quickly and freeze — like a statue!

  "GO" Move right or left with the ball, fast, for three or four yards.

  "TURN" Turn 180 degrees quickly with the ball and move three or four yards.

Teaching points

- Encourage players to keep the ball close to their feet.

- Occasionally insist on using left foot only or right foot only.

- Encourage players to keep their heads up while playing.

- See how many different ways they can turn with the ball.

- When introducing the instructions, do so one at a time with practice in between to avoid giving players too much at once.

- Later, incorporate your own ideas.

Target

- Stay in the area with the ball.

- No contact with other players or with other balls.

The Corner Shot

Objective

To develop accurate passing and shooting with both feet, and gain a simple understanding of corner kicks.

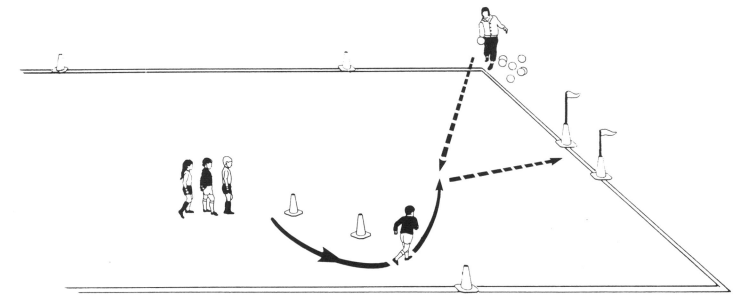

Organization

- Place balls at corners of playing area.

- Coach rolls ball by foot or by hand.

- Coach shouts "Go!" — player at first cone must go around second cone.

- Coach rolls ball as player comes around second cone.

- Shooting player goes behind goal to retrieve next shot, then returns to end of line.

- No goalkeepers, so players practice accurate kicking.

- Change players and cones to opposite side.

- Progression — players take corner kick themselves with simple rotation of players, but this is more difficult, so let them master the simpler practice first.

Teaching points

- As they become better, narrow the goal or deliver quicker passes.

- Point out that most shots in illustration will be taken left-footed. When practice is switched, they will be predominantly right-footed.

- Total concentration — head down, with eye on the ball.

- Encourage *accuracy* rather than stressing power shooting.

- Use inside of foot, like a hockey stick.

- Encourage players to strive to become "two-footed."

Target

- To record the number of the team's scoring attempts that succeed in 20 shots, and keep score for each practice.

Mack I

Objective

To develop passing and shooting skills with both feet and to teach the proper techniques for throw-ins.

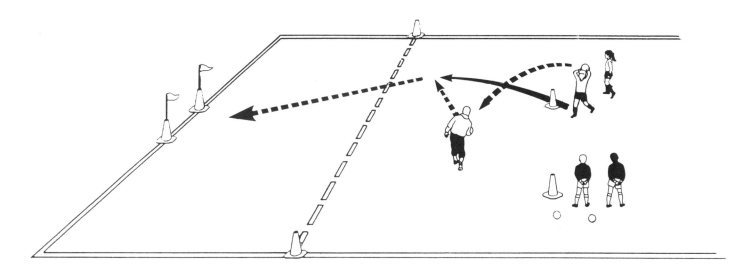

Organization

- Two marker cones placed five yards in from each sideline 15 yards from the goal.

- No goalkeeper and goals may be narrowed.

- First player on right "throws-in" to coach, who rolls ball for a first-time, right-footed shot.

- Player retrieves ball, then goes to back of the left line.

- First player at left marker cone does same exercise but shoots with left foot, retrieves ball and goes to back of the right line.

Teaching points

- No goalkeeper, so players don't sacrifice accuracy for power and poor technique.

- Encourage careful, accurate shooting.

- For weaker players, roll ball closer to goal.

- As all players improve, roll ball at 90-degree angle or greater, or move cones back to force more power in shot without losing accuracy.

- Don't change practice conditions too soon. Each team should try beating its "record".

Target

- How many of 20 shots by the "team" are successful — record results for future competition.

Mack I and Mack II are named after John McKenzie, who helped develop both practices.

Mack II

Objective

To develop the skills of ball control while practicing the throw-in technique and kicking with both feet.

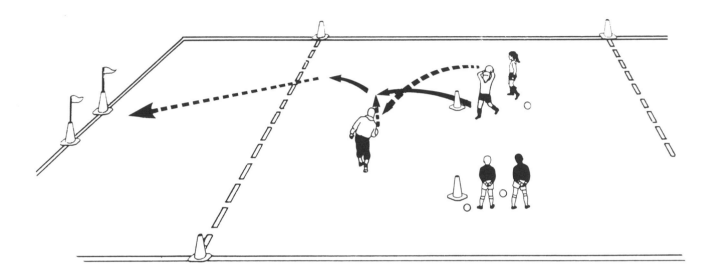

Organization

- Identical practice to the Mack I except every player must control the ball first before shooting. Shot must be left-footed from left, right-footed from right.

- Coach may vary his service to encourage different types of controlling touches:
  a) Initial practices — roll ball for ground control;
  b) Later, bounce or roll ball quickly at the incoming player to force quick decisions regarding the controlling surface;
  c) Serve ball in the air for control with thigh, chest or foot.

Teaching points

- The controlling touches can be affected with foot or any part of the body except hands.

- The shot must be with the right from the right, and with the left from the left. Therefore, control ball to the appropriate side to provide an angle for shot.

- Cushion ball with part of body controlling the ball.

- Encourage "two-touch" play — the first to control, the second to shoot, whenever possible. But don't make it compulsory.

- This is a much more difficult exercise than MACK I, so allow players as many touches as they need before shooting with the right or left foot, whichever is required.

Target

- To control the ball and to score; keeping of results optional.

Goalie I

Objective

To give all players the opportunity to become comfortable handling a ball by throwing and catching.

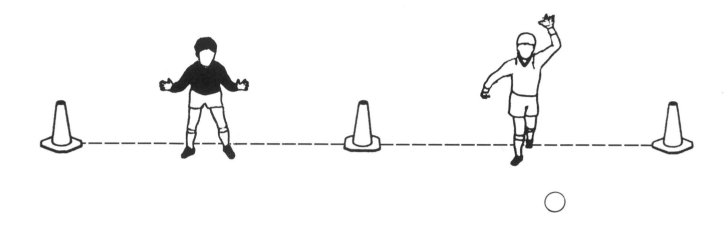

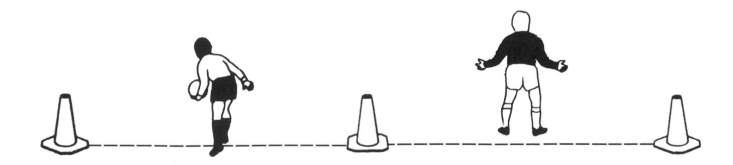

Organization

- Players in pairs, five to six yards apart, throwing and lobbing to each other.

- If possible, use cones or markers to improvise goals for each pair.

- Consider using this practice as part of warmup with the Square Dance.

Teaching points

- Have players reach forward to catch ball with fingers and palms.

- After catching, bring the ball into body to hide it.

- Players should treat the ball as a friend — to be hugged, not pushed away.

Target

- To test your partners without beating them or forcing them to dive.

Goalie II
The Pendulum Roll

Objective

To introduce players to the all-important technique of diving to either side.

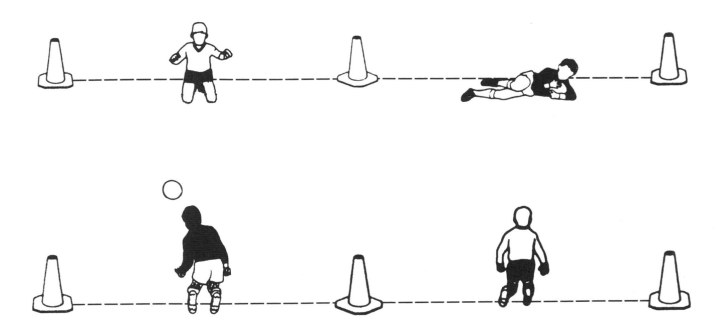

Organization

- Two players kneel in an upright position, facing one another four yards apart.

- Ball is rolled two to four feet to either side.

- Player receiving the ball rolls sideways, collects the ball and rolls back to the kneeling position with the ball.

- Once back in the upright kneeling position, the sequence is repeated for the second player.

- Players should be encouraged to roll the ball to both sides of their partner — but not necessarily systematically.

- Use as part of warm-up.

Teaching points

- Roll on side, not stomach or back.

- Receive the ball with hands and arms in front of body.

- Pull ball into midriff (see Goalie I).

- Roll from side-diving position back to kneeling position.

Target

- Ten rolls (five for each player), with continuous pendulum action.

Goalie III

Objective

To make players familiar with the techniques of diving saves from an upright position, and to relieve the fear of tumbling.

Organization

- Two small goals, nine feet wide using cones or markers, approximately eight yards from each other.

- Players kick or throw ball to "test" rather than to beat opponent.

- Ground shots to the side result in practice for diving saves.

- Use as separate practice, not as part of the warm-up.

- Practice in grassy or sandy area.

Teaching points

- Goalkeeper must be alert and 'dancing' in readiness for a shot.

- For longer dives to the side, a short sideways skip precedes diving.

- Keep as much of the body behind the ball as possible — double cover with hands and some part of the body.

- Ensure 'shots' are good, yet varied.

- Review Teaching Points in Goalie I and II, particularly "side-diving".

Target

- Ten shots (five each), then rest.

The Numbers Game

Objective

To develop good attacking and defending skills in a "fun game" practice and to use 1 vs 1 and 2 vs 2 as the learning situation.

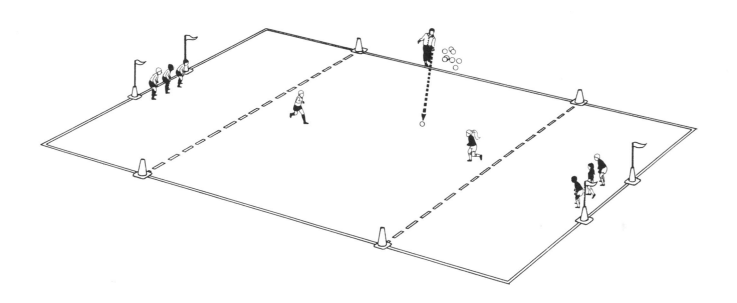

Organization

- Use the 3-a-side *Micro Soccer* field.

- Widen the goals.

- All players start on goal line.

- Each player on each team is given a number.

- Coach calls out number. . . e.g. "three". . . and rolls the ball into play.

- The two opposing number 'three' players leave the goal line immediately and compete for possession for a maximum of 20 seconds.

- Coach keeps the balls by him and rolls another ball into play if one is kicked out.

- Call two numbers — "one" and "three" — to create 2 vs 2.

- Remaining players defend goal, without using hands, and must stay within one yard of goal line.

- If one player fails to respond to the number, a penalty is called — a free shot at open goal from half-way line, to keep players on their toes and make it fun.

Teaching points

- If organization is working, let them play, enjoy the game and learn by trial and error.

- Encourage attackers to take on opponents and *Go for Goal!*

- Defenders should stay on their feet as long as possible, rather than slide-tackling.

- Defenders must run back even when beaten.

Target

- To outscore opposing team.

Beach Head

Objective

To teach the technique of heading in a way that is fun — and painless!

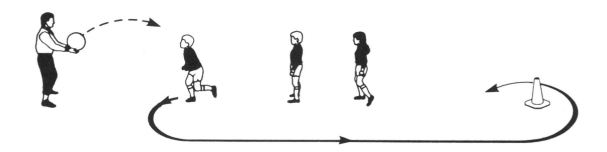

Organization

- Use a beach ball, or a slightly-deflated, hand-stitched leather ball.

- Stand players in line in front of coach — the first player three yards away.

- Ball is thrown underhand to head of first player, who heads it back to coach's face and runs around marker to join back of line.

- Everyone sits down cross-legged when last player is finishing.

- If assistance is available, have two or three teams competing.

Teaching points

- Players must keep eyes open and watch ball onto head.

- Use the forehead to head the ball.

- Heading ball back to thrower's face will help produce the right technique.

- Never use plastic or laminated balls, because they hurt.

Target

- If there's only one team, coach clocks procedure to set a *record*.

- If two or more teams, first to finish with all players sitting cross-legged wins.

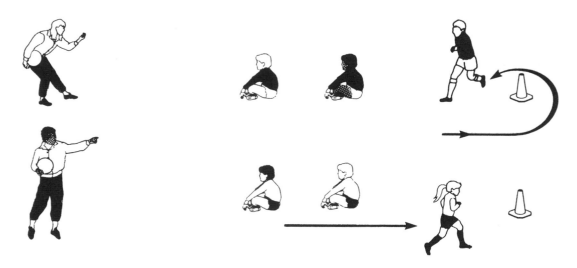

Change Soccer

Objective

To involve every player in a 2 vs 2 or 3 vs 3 fun game emphasizing co-operation and skills development.

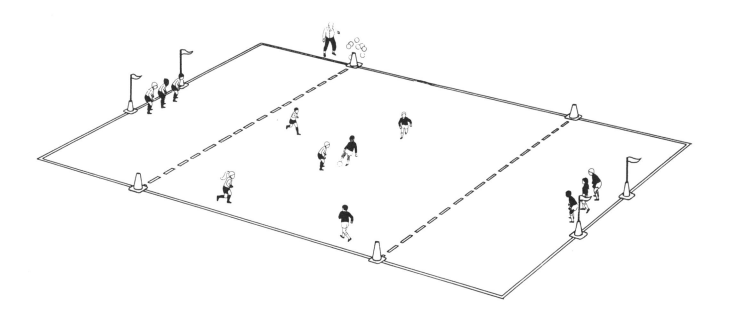

Organization

- Group is split into two; if odd number, coach joins in or plays strongest squad a player short.

- In the example shown, three players from each team play a normal game.

- Three players on each team are collective goalkeepers — no handling and positioned no more than two yards off each goal line.

- Coach shouts "Change!" and on-field teams run back to goal line without touching the ball again — and to become the "goalkeepers".

- "Goalkeeping" teams become the on-field teams and move quickly to win possession.

- Coach shouts "Change!" at any time.

- Make goals wide enough so that it's not too difficult to score.

- Any major infraction means a free shot from half-way line, with no goalkeepers.

Teaching points

- Encourage players to pass frequently in order to create scoring chances.

- Encourage "goalkeeping team" to move sideways together, as a wall.

- Defenders should help each other and should stay on their feet as much as possible.

Target

- To outscore the opposition.

Guidelines for a *Micro Soccer* practice session

Length: 30 – 45 minutes maximum.

Spend at least half of practice session in game form: (a) 3-a-side
  (b) Numbers game
  (c) Change soccer

Start with *Square Dance*, to get players "bubbling".

Use a goalkeeping practice at least every other week — usually as a part of warm-up.

Use only one skills practice per session: (a) Mack I
  (b) Mack II
  (c) Corner Shot
  (d) Beach Head

Occasionally use fun games or exercises — even if not soccer related — as a change of pace.

CAUTION:

Do not try to cram all the practices outlined in this segment into too short a period of time. Some practices suggested may not be used until next season!

Remember, in skills development, continuity and repetition are important. But don't bore the kids, either! There is a fine balance to be achieved by coaches.

Structured spontaneity

In the mining villages of Durham and Northumberland in the northeast of England, they used to say that if you needed a soccer player, go to the pit head and whistle, and three center forwards would appear.

This was one of England's great breeding grounds of high quality soccer players. The "Northeast", particularly in the '30s, was a depressed area with high unemployment. There was little to do. So the kids and the young men played soccer morning, noon and night.

Similar conditions have been prevalent in the other soccer breeding grounds of the world, such as in Europe and South America. Those conditions also continue today in some parts of South America and in the emerging soccer nations of Africa.

Given those circumstances, where do the kids learn their soccer skills? Not by coaching! They play small-sided soccer — 2-a-side, 3-a-side, 4-a-side — almost always with an improvised soccer field and often with an improvised soccer ball.

It is from this kind of environment that most of the great players have emerged. . . along with the average player who was still highly skilled in the basics of the game. Generally speaking, those conditions do not exist in North America — and no longer exist in Europe. But the requirement to have fun, kick the ball and develop skills most certainly does.

How to do it? By "structured spontaneity". This play on words is indeed a contradiction of terms, but it is one for a purpose. Coaches need to re-create the conditions under which kids had great fun and learned the game. This is the purpose of *Micro Soccer*.

Sample practice schedule

For a group of 10 to 12 players, 7 years old

WEEK 1

Square Dance	10 minutes
3-a-side game	10 minutes
Mack I	7 minutes
3-a-side game	10 minutes
TOTAL	37 minutes

WEEK 2

Goalie I	5 minutes
Square Dance	7 minutes
Change Soccer	9 minutes
Mack I	7 minutes
3-a-side	9 minutes
TOTAL	37 minutes

WEEK 3

Goalie II	5 minutes
Square Dance	7 minutes
3-a-side	10 minutes
Numbers Game	10 minutes
3-a-side	5 minutes
TOTAL	37 minutes

WEEK 4

Square Dance	10 minutes
3-a-side	10 minutes
Mack I	7 minutes
Change Soccer	10 minutes
TOTAL	37 minutes

WEEK 5

Goalie I, II, III	12 minutes
3-a-side	10 minutes
Mack II	10 minutes
3-a-side	7 minutes
TOTAL	39 minutes

WEEK 6

Square Dance	7 minutes
Change Soccer	9 minutes
Mack II	8 minutes
Numbers Game	8 minutes
3-a-side	7 minutes
TOTAL	39 minutes

WEEK 7

Square Dance	10 minutes
3-a-side tournament	25 minutes
TOTAL	35 minutes

WEEK 8

Goalie I, II, III	10 minutes
Corner Shot	10 minutes
Numbers Game	8 minutes
3-a-side	10 minutes
TOTAL	38 minutes

To have fun, be flexible!

Be prepared to change the program if things are not going well. Use any fun activity just to get the children 'bubbling' again.

ROLES in *Micro Soccer*

The Goalkeeper

The goalkeeper plays a vital role in the success of "team play" in 3-a-side soccer, including the offensive plays. The coach should encourage the goalkeeper to think in terms of becoming a goalkeeper *and* supporting defender.

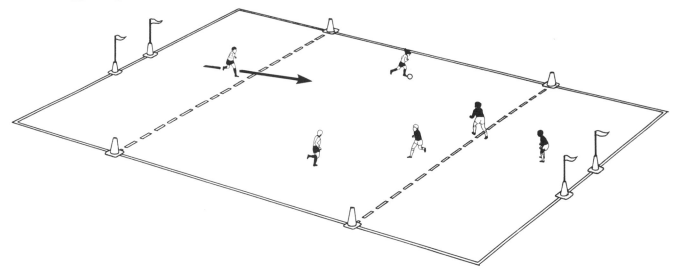

The goalkeeper moving outside his zone to give rear support

In providing effective rear support, the goalkeeper must do so without venturing so far he puts his team at risk. He has to always keep in mind that he is the only one who can handle the ball.

But there is no reason why he cannot move in support outside the handling zone, and move backwards to the goal when the opposition wins possession.

The goalkeeper should be made aware of the fact he can use his feet outside the handling zone.

Players just starting out, or when first introduced to Micro Soccer, will not immediately comprehend the total role of the goalkeeper in Micro Soccer. Initially, goalkeepers will tend to remain on the goal line, and the game will, in effect, be 2 vs 2 plus 2 goalkeepers. There is nothing wrong with this. Let the children develop with the game. Over a period of 12/24 months, with the encouragement of the coach, the fuller goalkeeping role will become more evident.

The Supporting Attacker

With one attacker in possession of the ball and the goalkeeper giving *rear support*, the other player becomes the *supporting attacker* — with emphasis on *attack*. This player should be encouraged to make adventuresome runs into space to receive the ball in advanced attacking positions.

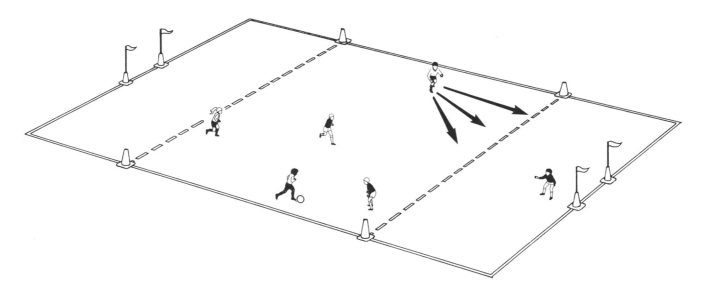

Supporting attacker going forward

Or . . .

The supporting attacker can look to move towards the player with the ball to work a passing movement to create a scoring chance.

This is termed *attacking support* or *forward support*.

ON THROW-INS:

Normally on throw-ins, the goalkeeper gives the rear or defensive support.

The supporting attacker should think in positive terms — how to receive the ball in an advanced and a potential scoring position (see "re-starts").

Supporting attacker's role on throw-ins

ON CORNER KICKS:

The supporting attacker can make an adventuresome run to co-operate with the corner kicker to create a shooting opportunity.

Supporting attacker's role on corner kicks

Player with the Ball

Assuming the player in possession of the ball is not the goalkeeper and that the goalkeeper is giving rear support, the player should be encouraged to make decisions from the options normally presented:

1. "Go for Goal" — the player looks to score by dribbling and running past opponents.
2. Shooting, if the opportunity is there.
3. Combining with the supporting attacker on passing moves towards the goal.

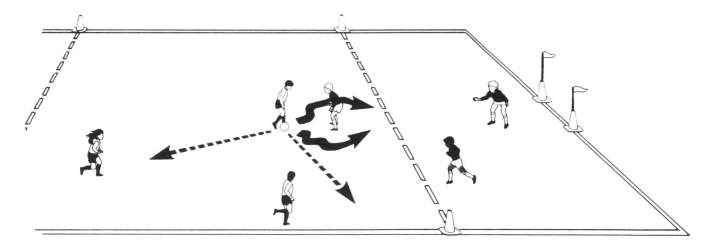

Exciting options for player with ball

In 3-a-side, these options will be obvious and players should be encouraged — not criticized — if they make a choice that fails.

A further option is to pass the ball back to the rear supporting player, normally the goalkeeper. This should be pointed out as a *real* option, but with greater encouragement to look for the more positive forward options *first*.

Children learn by doing. Let them *do* it, enjoy it and learn it, by trial and error.

The Coach

Because 3-a-side will give every player lots of ball contact, and because of small numbers and the simple nature of the game, the best teacher *is* the game. Children will learn by playing.

The coach can do a first-class job by *organizing* and *supervising* the practice and then *encouraging* and *praising* the players. Of course, if the coach is confident of his information, he can also help the players make tactical decisions by encouraging actions.

Be cautious! An often-used expression in the north of England is: "If in doubt say nowt!" In *North American* English: "If you are unsure of your facts, don't say a word!"

In the next segment is a summary of the tactical considerations — to help the coach understand how players can become a more effective unit.

But don't feel the onus is on you to coach. Organize and supervise . . . and let them play.

Variations on the *Micro Soccer* theme

Micro Soccer has been developed as a microcosm of the international game. It has the philosophy that the game is born, and develops and progresses, from this base. It includes the essential ingredients of soccer — goalkeepers, throw-ins, corner kicks and supporting players. But don't get locked into the rules and organization recommended earlier in the manual. For instance, on a cool day or for a change of pace, why not dispense with a goalkeeper, narrow the goals and play 3-a-side with no handling?

With a large group of 18 or more and with only one coach, you can split the group into three teams of six or seven. Then play one mod/mini game on one field, i.e. . . 6-a-side, preferably with a parent supervising while you conduct a 3-a-side game on an adjacent field. Every five or 10 minutes, rotate the teams so that each team has equal time in each activity.

Variety is the spice of life but flexibility and innovation are good coaching qualities, too.

TACTICS of *Micro Soccer*

The respective attacking roles of the three players in *Micro Soccer* — the goalkeeper or rear defender, the player in possesssion of the ball and the supporting attacker — have already been outlined. So have some of the expectations and possibilities on throw-ins and corner kicks.

To highlight the *tactical considerations* of the 3-a-side game, look closely at the "re-start" circumstances of *Micro Soccer*.

Re-starts

The term "re-start" is used in all situations where the game begins, or when it starts again. This can be following a stoppage, or at the beginning of the game, or after half-time. They are also described as "dead ball situations". Both corner kicks and throw-ins are re-starts. So, too, are free kicks and goal kicks.

A penalty kick is a "re-start" but there should be no such award in *Micro Soccer* — only free kicks after an infringement such as handling or tripping. Penalties are too severe a punishment at this age and should not be introduced until later.

All free kicks should be "indirect" — the ball must be passed first before a shot can be taken at the goal — because it forces the players to think in terms of passing and, therefore, co-operating.

This **co-operation** should be the underlying theme in the three "re-starts" to be examined in more detail: the *goal kick*, the *throw-in* and the *corner kick*. These re-start situations require some teaching if young players are to understand how to take advantage of possession.

In the adult game, opposing players must stand at least 10 yards from the ball at free kicks and corner kicks. That's inappropriate in *Micro Soccer* so a "five-yard rule" is used on goal kick, free kick and corner kick situations.

Note: Opponents are allowed to be at any distance they choose on throw-ins.

Corner Kicks

Because of the small size of the field, the corner kick in *Micro Soccer* becomes an especially-important re-start. For example, on a corner kick with larger numbers and bigger fields, the young kicker does not possess the strength to kick the ball into the goal area.

The corner kick in *Micro Soccer* is an exercise in:

  (a) Accurate passing by the kicker.
  (b) "Timing of the run" by the receiver.

34

(c) Positional awareness by both the supporting attacker and the rear supporting player (the goalkeeper).

(d) Shooting at goal.

(e) Developing an *understanding* between the kicker and receiver.

The corner kick is a meaningful component of *Micro Soccer*.

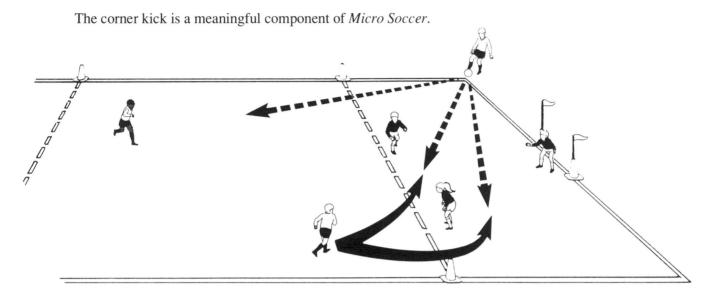

Some attacking options on corner kicks

Goal Kicks

The goalkeeper is allowed to take a goal kick from anywhere inside his handling zone. It is to his advantage to take the kick from the front of the goalkeeping zone to gain a six-yard advantage. The ball is placed on the ground and must be stationary when kicked.

The goalkeeper should be encouraged to produce a positive attacking situation from the kick, rather than just booting it forward and hoping.

The effectiveness of the goal kick will depend to a great extent on the two outfield players. These two players should take *wide positions* on opposing sides as a starting point.

This presents the greatest number of options for the attacking team. Initially, the two attacking players should not be too close to their goalkeeper, nor so far up-field as to make it difficult for the goalkeeper to find one of them. Half-way is a good rule-of-thumb.

These are the goalkeeper's options:

1. A kick down the middle for both wide players to run on to, for a shot at goal.
2. An angled goal-kick pass to the feet of an unmarked wide player.
3. A kick to a player short of the middle but still holding the wide position. Or, from the same move . . .
4. A ball played into the space created by the player who has run short, enabling the third player to make a diagonal run forward for a longer kick from the goalkeeper.

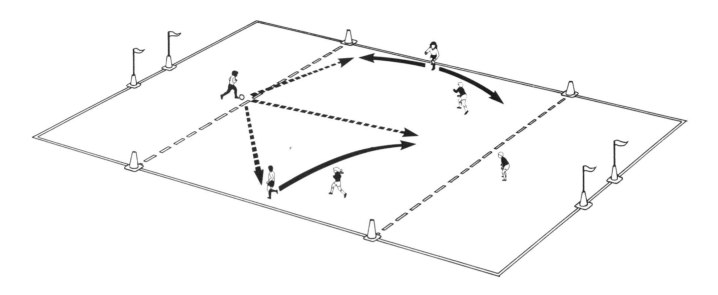

Options for players going wide on goal kicks

Note:

1. Do not be overly concerned about coaching the different options as long as players are encouraged to *split wide* into the initial starting positions. The different options will become apparent to the players as they play and learn by trial and error.

2. When a goalkeeper gathers the ball in his hands during fluid play, this does not result in a goal kick (i.e. a dead ball situation). The goalkeeper should play the ball either with a kick from his hands, by a throwing pass or by bringing the ball forward out of the goal area with his feet to start an attack. However, the same thinking should apply with the two outfield players regarding positioning — split wide to give the attacking goalkeeper *options*.

Throw-ins

This particular re-start often presents the most difficulties to young players. Since they have to master the throw-in technique, it's strongly recommended the *Mack I* and *Mack II* practices are used on a regular basis.

On a throw-in, the same understanding should be applied as on the corner kick. That is, one positive-thinking attacking player is trying to:

(a) Make forward runs, or
(b) Receive the ball in a forward position.

The "forward-thinking" player should be secure in the knowledge there is a "rear supporting player" — the goalkeeper — covering up for him.

The diagram suggests simple but effective options available to the thrower. Success will depend on the understanding developed by *all three* players.

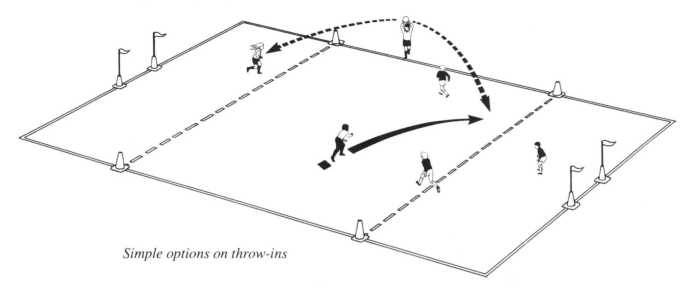

Simple options on throw-ins

OPTION 1
Ball is thrown into the striking area, to arrive at the same time as supporting player making a forward run, for a shot at the goal.

OPTION 2
A safe throw, to rear supporting defender (goalkeeper), possibly into player's hands.

OPTION 3
A ball thrown forwards *down the line* for supporting attacker to turn and go for the goal.

OPTION 4
Ball is thrown to the feet of the attacking player in an advanced position who can either turn and shoot or combine with the thrower moving up in support.

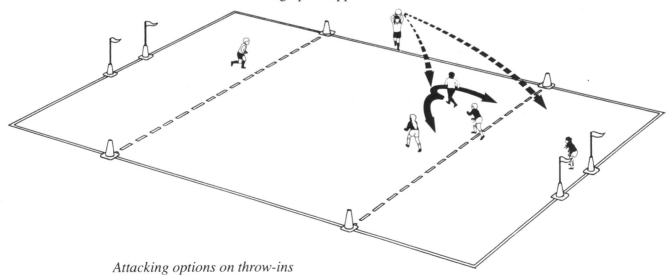

Attacking options on throw-ins

Fluid Play

Understanding the expectations and opportunities of the three roles of *Micro Soccer* — that of the goalkeeper and each of the two outfield players — will result in *combined play* in the normal flow of the game. This is where the *Micro* practices and the *Micro* game are the teachers.

Of course, the role of each player will change as the ball is passed and as different players gain or regain possession. This will be particularly true of the two outfield players as the *flying* goalkeeper role is more structured.

Remember, this is only three players per team — a situation the players can handle, learn from and enjoy!

Defending

There is no need for a coach to emphasize defending at this age. Players in *Micro Soccer* will defend naturally and, normally, very well.

Two aspects, however, should be encouraged:

1. After losing the ball and/or when the opposing team has possession, each player should run back to help out teammates.

2. Players should defend as much as possible standing up, not falling in desperation.

Conclusion

To the Coach

This tactical summary of *Micro Soccer* and its practices is included in this segment to help broaden the coach's knowledge. Do not feel that all this knowledge must be passed on to young players. A coach's main role is to organize, supervise, encourage and praise players. Only when the coach fully understands the information should he attempt to *coach* the players.

Let them play.

Don't go to 4-a-side without a valid reason

Variety and flexibility are key considerations when coaching this age group but so is caution. Don't move from 3-a-side to 4-a-side game just because it occupies another player on the team. That may still be a valid reason but you need to examine your motives for increasing the numbers.

The 3-a-side game is soccer's base. Every player in 3-a-side has a key role. The fourth player may become a "spare"; he could even opt out without seriously damaging the team unit. He may find, as could others, the duplication of roles initially confusing. Sooner or later, all players are going to progress in terms of numbers and the space until ultimately they graduate to the 11-a-side game.

But progress must be for the right reasons and at the right time.

THE HOWE WAY

By Bobby Howe

The beauty of the game of soccer is its simplicity. Within a given set of rules, there are two teams whose objective is to score goals. Each team consists of 11 players who must combine individual abilities cohesively to try to win the game. Within a game there are individual and small group games which have to be won for the whole team to succeed.

The game presents a series of motor and sensory-motor challenges. Having control of the body while being in control of the ball is essential to a player's success. Unlike golf, where skill can be improved by repetition of the correct technique, soccer is a game with skills that can only be improved by exposure to the demands of the game — movement of the ball, movement of the body with the ball and opposing pressure.

Psychologically, young players of 6, 7, and 8 years of age are unable to cope with the decision-making necessary to play 11-a-side soccer. At that age, they are also incapable of sharing the ball with many teammates. It is important, therefore, that coaches do not present such unrealistic challenges or ask for such decisions.

As small-sided games are the foundation upon which the 11-a-side game is based, it is important that players are exposed to small-sided games at an early age. The younger the age, the fewer number of players that should be involved. Fewer numbers create more touches of the ball, easier decisions, greater enjoyment and more learning for the player.

The examples in this segment are games which allow players to be exposed to the elements of soccer without the necessity of much information from the coach. Individual player performance will improve through using the following elements of the game in practice:

(1) The ball

(2) The field of play

(3) An objective

(4) An opponent

(5) A teammate

(6) Rules

(7) Direction

(8) Decision making

In many cases, parents volunteer or are volunteered to act as coaches when their children start to play. For parents who have limited or no playing experience, the position of coach can be quite intimidating. Perhaps some of the fear can be removed if the coach understands that young players learn more from games than from the coach.

The game is *The Great Teacher*.

Game One

A fun dribbling activity using four corners or target areas

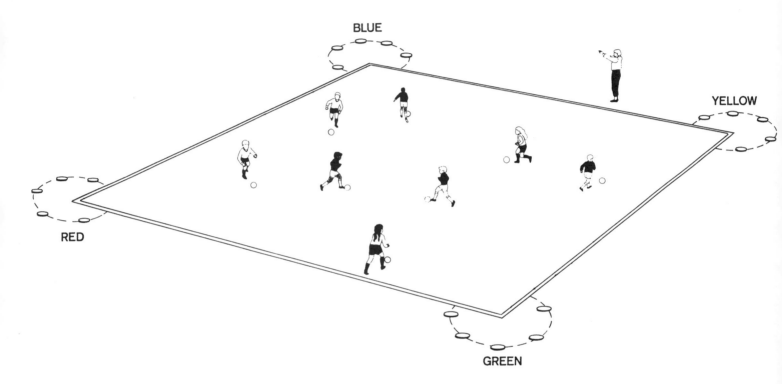

Game Rules

- Eight players with a ball each dribble inside the marked area shown (20 yards by 20 yards).
- Four additional areas are marked on the outside of each corner with frisbees or cones, and are designated as being the red, yellow, green and blue areas.
- Each player tries to prevent the ball rolling into another player or another player's ball.
- All players try to keep within the marked area at all times.
- On the command "Stop!", the players freeze with one foot on top of the ball.
- On the command "Red!" or "Yellow!" or "Green!" or "Blue!", the players dribble quickly to the appropriate corner while trying to avoid other players.

Player Objectives

- Maintain control of the ball, manipulating the ball to avoid collisions.
- Develop changes of speed and direction.
- Keep the head up to see the other players while looking down to see the ball.

Game Two

A fun dribbling game introducing the aspect of shielding the ball

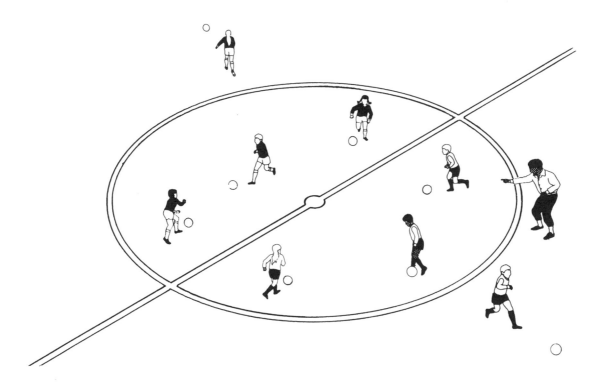

Game Rules

- Eight players with a ball each dribble inside the center circle.
- Each player manipulates and protects the ball but also tries to kick other balls outside the circle.
- If a player's ball is kicked out, player retrieves it quickly and continues with the game.
- A player may only attempt to kick another player's ball while in possession of his/her own; if his/her own ball has been kicked out of the circle, player may not kick another's ball.
- A player is eliminated when the ball is kicked out of the circle three times.
- The winner is the only player who does not have a ball kicked out three times.

Player Objectives

- Shield the ball — keep the body between the ball and challenging players.
- Keep control of the ball, turn with it and accelerate with it to avoid a challenge.
- Keep the head up to see the other players while looking down to see the ball.

Game Three

A 1 vs 1 dribbling game with goal areas to attack and defend

Game Rules

- Place five sets of goals (made with cones) around the center circle as shown in diagram.
- Make each goal two yards wide.
- Divide eight players into four pairs; one player of each pair with the ball, the other an opponent.
- The player with the ball tries to maintain possession under pressure from the opponent and tries to score through any of the five sets of goals.
- While the area outside the center circle may be used, a goal is scored from only inside the area.
- To score, the player must dribble the ball through one of the goals — but may not pass the ball through — and successfully maintain possession.
- A loss of possession occurs when the player: a) loses the ball to opponent; b) allows the ball to collide with any other ball in the playing area; c) collides with a goalpost while trying to score; d) passes the ball through a goal rather than dribbling.
- The score is kept in each 1 vs 1 duel.
- The game should be no longer than two minutes before allowing players to rest, because the 1 vs 1 nature of the game presents great physical demands. Quality of play deteriorates as players become fatigued. It is important they are given time to recover.

Player Objectives

- Maintain control under the pressure of opposition, keeping the body between the ball and the opponents.
- Turn away from the opponent and not into the opponent.
- Change direction and pace.
- Keep an eye on the ball, but with head up to avoid collision and to see which goal is open.

Game Four

A passing, dribbling and shooting game where one side is given an extra player (2 vs 1)

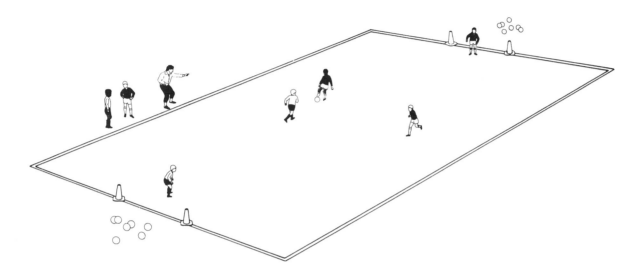

Game Rules

- Have substitute players to replace those who are playing.
- One team has a single outfield player; the other, two; and both a goalkeeper.
- Several balls should be kept behind each goal to keep a ball in play quickly.
- Make the goal four yards wide, and create a play area 25 yards by 15 yards.
- Encourage *both* teams to score even though one has a manpower advantage.
- When the ball is out of play, start the game at the goal line by the goalkeeper.
- A ball in play *cannot* be played back to the goalkeeper.
- Keep score.

Player Objectives

- Watch the ball but keep head up to observe opponents and the goal.

TEAM WITH TWO OUTFIELD PLAYERS:
- The player in possession has two options — pass the ball or keep it.
- Pass to teammate with pace and accuracy, and use teamwork to score.
- For the player not in possession, support teammate by being visible.

TEAM WITH ONE OUTFIELD PLAYER:
- Player in possession keeps the ball until the angle to shoot exists, then tries to score.
- Manipulate ball, keeping body between opponents and the ball.
- Change pace and direction.

Game Five

A 3-a-side game which emphasizes dribbling, passing and shooting

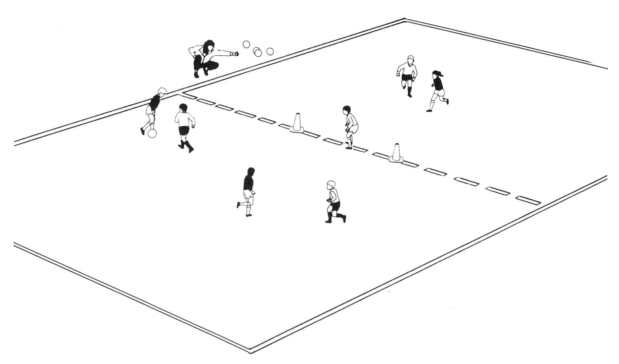

Games Rules

- A normal 3-a-side game in an area approximately 30 yards by 20 yards, except that it is played around one goal rather than towards two.

- Emphasize shooting at goal at the earliest opportunity.

- Players combine to create goal-scoring opportunities.

- Team in the dark uniforms can score only from the left side of the field, and team in white only from the right side.

- Re-start game with a throw-in any time the ball goes out of bounds.

- When goalkeeper makes a save from one team, he throws the ball into the opposing half of the field.

Player Objectives

- To take early shots from within shooting distance of the goal.

- To provide support for the player with the ball.

Game Six

A 1 vs 1 vs 1 game that induces the player in possession to create a shooting position

Game Rules

- One ball for three players in the area shown in the diagram, approximately 15 yards square.
- Each player plays against the other two players.
- Each player tries to score in a goal four to five yards wide.
- When the ball goes out of play, the coach puts another ball in play.
- Goalkeeper making a save throws the ball to the coach.
- After 10 balls are served, all three players and the goalkeeper are changed.
- Keep score, and play the winners against each other to name the champion.

Player Objectives

- Control the ball from the coach.
- Manipulate the ball to avoid challenges.
- Shield the ball when necessary.
- Change direction — turn with the ball.
- Change pace.
- Shoot at the earliest opportunity.

Game Seven

A 3 vs 2 game where the attackers have to combine to create scoring chances

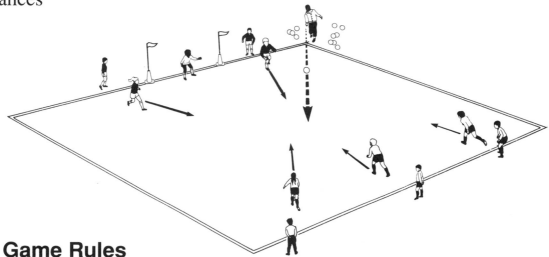

Game Rules

- Divide the players into two teams.
- Toss a coin to determine offensive team and defensive team.
- All the play takes place within the area shown — 20 yards by 15yards, with a goal five yards wide.
- Keep a large supply of balls.
- Play four minutes and then change to allow the defending team to attack and the attacking team to defend.
- Keep score.
- The coach starts the play by serving the ball to any of the three attackers at the front of a line.
- The three combine to score a goal.
- When the coach serves the ball, the two front defenders may leave their positions and try to prevent the attacking team from scoring.
- When a goal is scored or the goalkeeper makes a save or the ball goes out of play, the five players leave the area quickly to allow five more players to play.

Player Objectives

PLAYER WITH THE BALL:
- Control the ball from the coach.
- Manipulate the ball to avoid challenge.
- Shoot at the earliest good opportunity.

ATTACKING PLAYERS WITHOUT THE BALL:
- Support the player in possession of the ball.
- Know where and when to run so that a pass from the player with the ball cannot be intercepted.

Game Eight

A fun game which encourages good kicking technique and develops passing skills

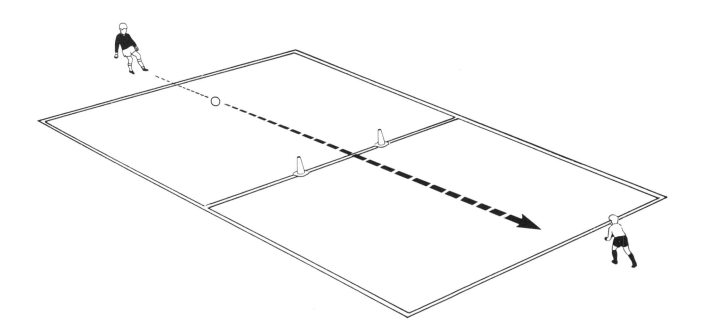

Game Rules

- Mark out an area approximately 15 yards by 10 yards with a goal three yards wide in the middle.
- Each player remains behind his own line.
- A shot can be played with the inside or outside of the foot through the goal.
- The receiving player controls the ball *behind* his line and tries to pass the ball through the goal (if by lack of control, the ball rebounds into the goal, it does not count).
- As the players improve, increase the length of the area or decrease the size of the goal.
- Limit the touches to three or, as the players improve, to two.
- Play the game for five minutes and have the players keep score.

Player Objectives

- To control the ball and set up the pass.
- To achieve pace and accuracy of passes.

Game Nine

A fun center circle practice that develops accurate kicking

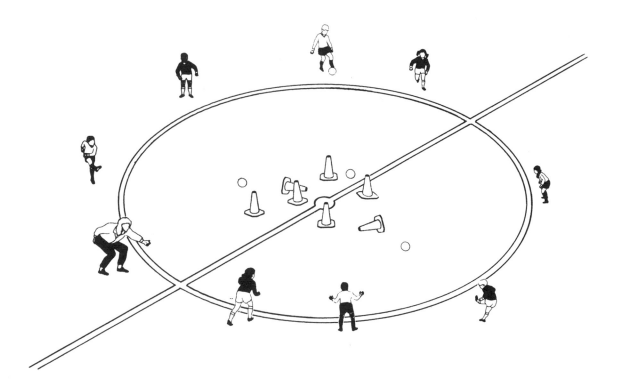

Game Rules

- Eight players on the outside of the center circle.
- Each player on one side of the circle has a partner directly opposite.
- Each pair has one ball between them.
- One player passes the ball towards partner but tries to knock over a cone in the center circle.
- The partner retrieves the ball and returns the pass through the center circle, again trying to knock over a cone.
- The ball must be passed from outside the circle.
- The game is stopped to pick up the cones.
- The winners are the pair to first knock over the cones 10 times.

Player Objective

- To achieve pace and accuracy of pass.

Game Ten

A fun circle game that develops combined passing and shooting

Game Rules

- Make the goal one cone placed inside an area with a radius of approximately six yards.
- If a liner is not available, the circumference can be marked out with frisbees, bibs or other cones.
- The team in dark uniforms plays against the team in white.
- A goal is scored when the ball is played from *outside* the area to knock over the cone.
- All players are allowed to run through the circle but no player is allowed to touch the ball in the circle.
- If any player touches the ball in the area, the opposing team has a free shot at the "goal" from the edge of the circle.
- Keep score.

Player Objectives

PLAYER IN POSSESSION:
- To keep an eye on the ball but keep the head up to observe teammates, opponents and the goal.
- To maintain possession of the ball by keeping the body between the ball and opponent.
- To change direction, by turning with the ball, and to change pace.
- To pass to teammates and choose which teammate is the better option.
- To achieve pace and accuracy of pass.

PLAYERS NOT IN POSSESSION:
- To support the player with the ball.
- To know where and when to run.
- To know not to make the same run as other supporting player or to crowd the player in possession of the ball.

NOTE: The game should be no longer than three minutes before allowing players to rest. The competitive 3-a-side nature of the game is physically demanding. Quality of play deteriorates as players become fatigued. It is important they have the opportunity to recover. With a group of 12, six play and six rest. Change frequently.

APPENDIX

RESPONSIBILITIES and EXPECTATIONS

The Coach

To dress appropriately and smartly.

To talk slowly and clearly.

To be on time for practices and games.

To plan practice sessions, and to plan for the game (pre-game instructions, substitute system).

To give players equal opportunity and equal time.

To encourage and be positive in correcting faults.

To have an adequate supply of balls and equipment.

To know emergency procedures — ambulance telephone numbers, first aid (carry a quarter).

To welcome other coaches and parents.

To be prepared to restrain, politely but firmly, overly-enthusiastic parents.

To be courteous to referees.

To listen to the players.

To organize the appointment of a team manager and help structure those responsibilities:
- Team list (with addresses and phone numbers)   • Cancellation procedure
- Practice and game schedule   • Club reporting systems   • Registrations

To know the rules of the game and to pass that knowledge on to young players.

To discuss player progress with parents.

To be capable of working miracles on a regular basis!!

The Parent

To make sure the player arrives at practices and games on time.

To ensure player is properly equipped with shoes, stockings, shin guards, shorts and jersey and, if required, sweats.

To stay at practice and games whenever possible — and to support your player and the team.

To help the coach wherever possible — perhaps assisting in practice, or participating — with the coach's agreement.

To inform coach and/or manager if player cannot attend practice or a game.

To encourage your child and team but not to insult or discourage the opposition.

To be enthusiastic, yet not critical.

To acknowledge the opposition's good plays.

To be sociable with the opposing team's parents.

To support, and not criticize, the referee.

To support, and not criticize, the coach.

To use mechanisms within the club if you think the coach is unsuitable.

To be positive and not let winning and losing change your attitude.

To be prepared to join a car pool.

To insist all children wear seat belts.

Above all, to let your child be what he or she is — a child.

The Manager

To produce team lists that include names of players and parents, home and business phone numbers, coach's and manager's names and phone numbers.

To look after registrations.

To make sure team has uniforms, balls and practice equipment.

To arrange practice locations and times, in conjunction with the coach.

To set up a phoning committee.

To establish half-time refreshment system for players (and parents).

To communicate as required with club officials.

To co-ordinate the cancellation procedures.

To establish referee system, including payment if necessary.

To communicate to parents the club insurance system — or lack of one!

To establish an emergency procedure in case of serious injury.

To arrange team activities.

To support the coach.

To influence the parents regarding their behaviour at games.

The Player

To bring a ball to practice, if required.

To keep soccer shoes clean.

To perform up to potential — but by the player's own standards, not those of the adults.

To get to practice on time (explain to Mom and Dad).

Rights of the player

To have equal playing opportunity — and the chance to score a goal (preferably in the opposing end!).

To enjoy, without undue pressure from the coach or parents, the world's most popular game.

HOW TO USE *Micro Soccer*

The Practice Session

Obviously, *Micro Soccer* and its practices can and should become an important component of the practice session for players in the 6, 7 and 8-year-old age group. This will guarantee the development of skill while preserving activity and entertainment considerations.

Encouragement should be given for the players to become familiar with the game and, particularly at the 8-year-old stage, to play 3-a-side soccer with their friends at home or at school.

At the team practice, if the numbers are greater than eight, the coach should consider using at least two fields.

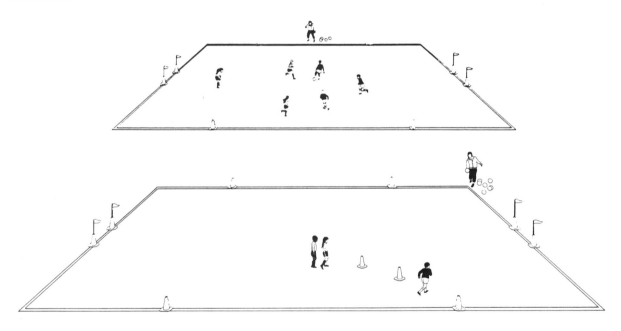

3-a-side game and corner shot practice

It should not be difficult to persuade a parent to assist. In the example shown with nine players at practice, one group of six is playing *Micro Soccer* while the other three players practice the Corner Shot. The practice group is rotated every six or seven minutes.

Twelve players become two groups of six. The coach organizes two 3-a-side areas and moves between each area spending time with each group in a skills practice while the other continues to play. Even in the absence of an assistant, it's surprising how well children play in a game with minimum supervision.

The Match-Day Formula

Some clubs have already introduced *Micro Soccer* for first-year players, as the start of the master plan.

One major advantage is that many players and teams can play on one standard-sized soccer field at the same time. It's a great way for kids (and parents) to begin their involvement with soccer — a jamboree-style competition each Saturday:

• With parents assisting and socializing.

• Where adjustments can quickly be made for the absence of a coach.

For clubs that consider implementing *Micro Soccer* as the inaugural game, consider the following:

Micro Soccer as the scheduled game

Team rosters of six (maximum) — ensuring at least 50 per cent playing time for everybody, with proper rotations.

Coaches take turns refereeing and timekeeping (or parents take on those responsibilities).

Time out is called every two minutes so that every player 'off-the-field' comes on for the next two minutes (see rotation system outlined on page 13).

Games are 36 minutes long (or as agreed by coaches); three periods of 12 minutes.

Line changes are made at the end of each period if numbers are six, so that the same players don't always play together.

'Foul throws' are corrected by referee and retaken by same player.

One team of six should have a co-team — with a plan of combining in future years as numbers on the field increase.

Co-teams practice at same time and same place, with the possibility of co-practice situations.

NOTE: In the first year, the game format and the scheduling need not be too structured, particularly if all teams are able to play at the same venue. Consider playing 6-a-side on the same area for the last six minutes of each game as a final "everyone-involved" fun finish. The quality of the game may not be as good but the experience will be pleasurable.

Some clubs for their own reasons may not want to make this innovative move and may wish to use *Micro Soccer* only as a practice system. It is a fact that almost twice as many coaches are required for 3-a-side with squads of six, as there would be for 7-a-side with squads of 10 to 12.

Nevertheless, it is our contention that many more parents will volunteer to coach *Micro Soccer* than 7-a-side, a contention confirmed by early experiences.

Why more volunteers?

1. The control problem of six as opposed to 10 to 12 is much less (even experienced school teachers are *tested* with large numbers in outdoor activities).

2. The simple formula of *Micro Soccer* plus this manual allows the coach to succeed by good organization and supervision even with little or no previous background in soccer.

Each club has to decide what works best for its own situation. Do you have to consider other clubs because of an interlocking program? Should boys and girls play together?* Can the club afford the additional expense in providing adequate equipment? Does the club prefer a more traditional philosophy when it comes to match play?

* The authors favour boys and girls playing together up to 10 years of age.

The Half-and-Half Formula

Most clubs schedule games on the weekend and designate at least one practice a week. This presents an opportunity for the best of both worlds.

The mid-week session can become the practice and play night (say, Wednesday) with every player in a certain age group (e.g. . . under 7) coming to one area. Remember that at least eight *Micro Soccer* fields can be marked on a standard-sized soccer field — accommodating up to 96 players.

A round-robin formula for 3-a-side games can be organized on a continuing week-by-week basis. During a 45-minute session, spend 15 minutes on the warm-up and one *Micro Soccer* practice and 30 minutes on the 3-a-side games.

If the teams are playing *Mod* or *Mini-Soccer* on the weekend, rosters of 12 are common. The weekend team should be split into two teams of six players for the *Micro* night with an assistant or parent looking after one team, and the regular coach the other.

The *Micro Soccer* practice-and-play night can be presented in many ways depending on the circumstances of the clubs.

The Tournament

A worthwhile consideration is to use the *Micro Soccer* formula periodically as a fun tournament. An example of a six-team tournament format is shown below:

Round One:	1 vs 2	3 vs 4	5 vs 6
Round Two:	2 vs 3	4 vs 5	1 vs 6
Round Three:	1 vs 3	2 vs 5	4 vs 6
Round Four:	1 vs 5	2 vs 4	3 vs 6
Round Five:	1 vs 4	3 vs 5	2 vs 6

Games of 12 minutes, allowing a full rotation with six players.
If five rounds is too long — play only three or four.

Elementary School

The physical education "games lesson" is an important part of any school curriculum. What better way for young children to have healthy recreation and exercise than *Micro Soccer* ? At the same time, they have the opportunity of learning ball skills and body co-ordination through soccer. However, the teacher normally has to deal with large numbers, as classes of 20–35 are common.

An example of how 32 (grade 3) children can be accommodated in a soccer "games lesson" of 40 minutes is shown below.

- Eight teams of 4 players.
- Two *Micro Soccer* fields, lined if possible, otherwise marked with frisbees or cones.
- One *Mod/Mini-Soccer* field, approximately 45 yards by 40 yards.
- Cones and flags to use as goals (12 of each).
- Minimum of three balls, but ideally many more.
- Teams change every eight minutes.

Round One:	A vs B, C vs D (*Micro*)
	E+F vs G+H (8-a-side)
Round Two:	E vs G, F vs H (*Micro*)
	A+B vs C+D (8-a-side)
Round Three:	A vs C, B vs D (*Micro*)
	E+G vs F+H (8-a-side)
Round Four:	E vs F, G vs H (*Micro*)
	A+C vs B+D (8-a-side)

For one teacher responsible for 32 children, there is limited opportunity to "coach". With assistance, the teacher could coach a *Micro* group each round and use one of the skills practices suggested in the manual. In these circumstances, the round-robin format would need some adjustment.

The Indoor Practice

Many coaches become concerned when they have to move indoors into a hall or gymnasium for an indoor practice. *Micro Soccer* and its practices will relieve that problem once and for all. All of the practice methods in this coaching manual are ideally suited for the indoor session. As well, most halls and gymnasia have the added advantage of lines already marked. One difficulty indoors is that normally the surface is hard (wood, composition, artificial turf) which makes the ball more lively and more likely to bounce. It is recommended that the balls are slightly deflated from the normal outdoor pressures.

PROGRESSIVE DEVELOPMENT

Soccer development — practice and play from age 6

Wipe the slate clean and start with the novice players at age 6, and develop them for the adult game. Consider the following, logical progression, inserted here to stimulate thinking and provoke reaction.

	Maximum squad	Players on field	Referee	Rules	Field size
Year 1 U7	6 plus co-team	3	Coach	No Offside	30 yards x 20 yards
Year 2 U8	6 plus co-team	3	Coach	No Offside	30 yards x 20 yards
Year 3 U9	6 plus co-team	4	Coach or Official	No Offside	35 yards x 25 yards
Year 4 U10	12 — Teams combine	6	Official	No Offside	45 yards x 30 yards
Year 5 U11	12	9	Official	No Offside	60 yards x 40 yards
Year 6 U12	15	11	Official	Offside	80 yards x 50 yards with FIFA markings

Comparing social, educational and soccer factors

Age	Natural friends and social groups	Soccer world wide, match play	Educational philosophy world wide	School class numbers
Under 6	2	5 to 11 a side	INFANT	
Under 8	2 or 3			
Under 10	3 or 4		JUNIOR	15
Under 12	3 or 4			to
Under 14	4 or 5	11 a side	SECONDARY	35
Under 16	5-plus			
Under 18	The "Gang"			

FUN ACTIVITIES

The philosophy in putting together this coaching manual was to identify the key considerations in coaching 6, 7 and 8-year-olds. We did not wish to make it too extensive and so risk losing sight of the most important factors. We have recognized "fun" and a change of pace and activity as being vital in stimulating young players.

Shown here are four "fun" practices taken from Karl Dewazien's excellent book, *Fundamental Soccer Practice*, as examples of fun soccer activities closely related to the game. Our recommendation is that each coach carries in his head five or six activities such as these which can be quickly introduced if a change of pace is desirable.

FOLLOW THE LEADER

Number of players:	Partners.
Equipment:	Each player with a ball.
Objective:	Mirror partner's moves.
Rules:	Imitate partner's moves.

Variation: Have the full team follow ONE leader.

CHAIN GANG

Number of players:	Three or more players linked by one hand on partner's shoulder.
Equipment:	One ball per linked group — "chain".
Objective:	Dribbling the ball without breaking the "chain".
Rules:	Once link is broken, go back to start.
Winners:	First "chain" to go through an obstacle course.
	First "chain" to go across a finish line.

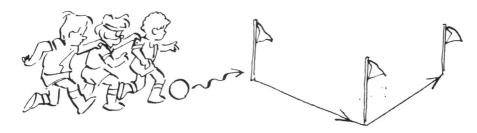

Variation: Soccer game of "chains" playing each other.

CAT & MOUSE (Group Game)

Number of players:	Full team.
Equipment:	All players have a ball — except "CAT".
Objective:	Be the last player to get caught.
Rules:	"CAT" calls for "MICE" to run from north to south or east to west across the sideline. When player is robbed of ball, the player also becomes a "CAT".
Winner:	Last "MOUSE" to have ball possession.

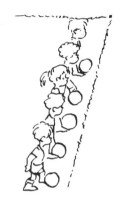 

Variation: "CAT" can call ONE player at a time from starting line.

VARIATION: CAT & MICE (Dodge Ball)

Number of players:	No limit.
Equipment:	One soccer ball per player, and one BIG marker.
Objective:	Not to get touched by the ball below the waist.
Rules:	One player "CAT" starts the game with ball. On signal from "CAT", the "MICE" run around the marker and back. "CAT" kicks ball at "MICE" and attempts to hit them below the waist. "MICE" that get hit by the ball (below the waist) become "CATS".
Winner:	Last player to get hit by the ball below the waist.

Reproduced with the author's permission from *Fundamental Soccer Practice*, by Karl Dewazien, State Youth Coach, California Youth Soccer Association —North.

THE ESSENTIAL SKILLS

"The giving and taking of passes is the essence of footba'." — Bill Shankly, 1970

Bill Shankly, the great architect and builder of the present Liverpool Football Club — the most successful club in the world over the past 30 years — made the game simple to his players and to everyone he met. To him, the giving of passes (kicking the ball) and the taking of passes (controlling the ball) were the two most important skills in the game of soccer, or footba' if you were brought up in Scotland.

In this illustration, the essential basic skills of the game are identified.

Essential skills

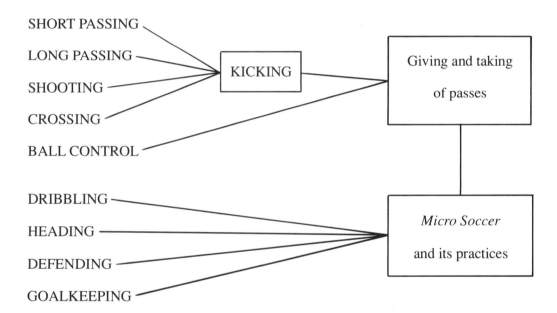

Micro Soccer and its practices place heavy emphasis on "the giving and taking of passes" and introduce the players to the other essential basics.

Important considerations

There are other basics, or fundamentals, for children playing soccer that need to be taken into account by coaches:

1. Environment — the correct playing and learning situation.
2. Kicks of the ball.
3. Being "on-the-team".
4. Playing — with others.
5. Understanding the game.

Micro Soccer attends to these needs, too.

3-A-SIDE ISN'T KIDS' STUFF

By Tony Waiters

When employed by the English Football Association, many of the coaches clinics I ran had to be held indoors in small gymnasia. I used 3-a-side soccer with the coaches to teach the principles of play. The importance of movement off the ball, supporting play, the use of the width of the field, penetration and improvisation could all be presented in the attacking aspect of 3-a-side soccer. Similarly, the principles of defense would be brought home vividly in 3-a- side play.

In the early 1970s, I joined Liverpool Football Club as their Youth Coach and immediately introduced a 3-a-side tournament formula for the 18 junior professionals, as a change of routine and as a learning activity every Wednesday. Bill Shankly, the Manager/Coach of Liverpool, used to watch what I was doing with the youth players carefully — out of interest but also out of care for his young players. He liked the 3-a-side tournament and asked me to include the senior professionals in future Wednesday tournaments. I was delighted and flattered. The great Shankly employing my methods! Or was he?

What I found out later was that when Bill Shankly was first appointed as Manager/Coach of Liverpool in the '60s, he introduced a number of new activities, one of which was 3-a-side soccer! But he structured the teams carefully. He teamed players like Chris Lawler, Tommy Smith and Ian Callaghan together. They played right defense, right midfield, right wing on the first team. Or Peter Thompson, Willy Stevenson and Roger Hunt — left wing, left midfield and striker. He knew that, within the team framework, the game was played in triangles and the team success would depend on how players playing around one another co-operated with and compensated for each other.

So, 3-a-side is not just kids' stuff. It's a great start for the kids but it has a place with players of every age, at every level. Whether you're coaching 6-year-olds, 7-year-olds, 8-year-olds, 18-year-olds or 28-year-olds consider 3-a-side as a valuable practice and development tool.

POSTSCRIPT

I stopped my car on Marine Drive in West Vancouver, British Columbia. I didn't have much choice. Two 6-year-old teams were playing 7-a-side soccer — *Mini-Soccer* as it's called in Canada. It was a beautiful October day with the last rays of summer warming parents sitting in picnic chairs on the sidelines. They were enthusiastically encouraging the two teams.

Two adults dominated the small soccer field towering above the players. They were the opposing coaches. Each was doing a terrific job but in different ways. The teams were not only in opposition — but in opposing tactical modes.

"Play position! Play position!" shouted the one coach as he pointed, cajoled and physically moved players into the places his team system demanded.

"Go for it guys! Go for goal! Well done, John! Come on, Tim!" yelled the other, as he enthusiastically encouraged his boys. His team had adopted the *swarm system* of play, not one devised by the coach, but one initiated by the enthusiasm of his team as they congregated around the ball hoping to kick it.

The *swarm* put a lock on the ball and moved like a giant amoeba towards the goal, opening up just enough for a shot — and a goal.

"Unlucky Tigers. . . get back to position!" shouted the losing coach. "John, stay on the right; Jeff, come on for Scott — play on the left defense. Let's go boys! Keep your positions. Play position, play position . . . .!"

It was to no avail.

The *swarm* snared the ball once more and took it — under cover — to the end of the field and scored again!

T. W.